Blockchain:

The Ultimate Beginner's Guide

Lee Maxwell

© 2016

TABLE OF CONTENT

Introduction

I want to thank you and congratulate you for downloading the book, "Blockchain: The Ultimate Beginner's Guide".

This book contains proven steps and strategies on BLOCKCHIAN.

A blockchain is a ledger of records arranged in data batches called blocks that use cryptographic validation to link themselves together. Put simply, each block references and identifies the previous block by a hashing function, forming an unbroken chain, hence the name.

Further Reading

Bitcoin firm bags first electronic money licence in the UK

Put like this, a blockchain just sounds like a kind of database with built-in validation—which it is. However, the clever bit is that the ledger is not stored in a master location or managed by any particular body. Instead, it is said to be distributed, existing on multiple computers at the same time in such a way that anybody with an interest can maintain a copy of it.

Better still, the block validation system ensures that nobody can tamper with the records. Rather, old transactions are preserved forever and new transactions are added to the ledger irreversibly. Anyone on the network can check the ledger and see the same transaction history as everyone else.

Effectively a blockchain is a kind of independent, transparent, and permanent database coexisting in multiple locations and shared by a community. This is why it's sometimes referred to as a mutual distributed ledger (MDL).

There's nothing new about MDLs, their origins traceable to the seminal 1976 Diffie–Hellman research paper New Directions In Cryptography. But for a long time they were regarded as complicated and not altogether safe.

It took the simpler blockchain implementation within Bitcoin to turn things around. The permanence, security, and distributed nature of Bitcoin ensured it was a currency maintained by a growing community but controlled by absolutely nobody and unable to be manipulated.

Further Reading

Bitcoin rival Ethereum fights for its survival after £30 million heist

Following the launch of Bitcoin, dozens of vigorous tech startups have vied with each other to produce the Next Big Thing in blockchain-based cryptocurrency, from the relatively-well-regarded Ethereum to the frankly ludicrous Coinye West.

A notable drawback of blockchains is that their distributed nature demands constant computational power in many multiple locations, and all the on-going accumulated (electrical) power that entails.

Thanks again for downloading this book, I hope you enjoy it!

Chapter 1

What is a 'Blockchain'

A blockchain is a public ledger of all Bitcoin transactions that have ever been executed. It is constantly growing as 'completed' blocks are added to it with a new set of recordings. The blocks are added to the blockchain in a linear, chronological order. Each node (computer connected to the Bitcoin network using a client that performs the task of validating and relaying transactions) gets a copy of the blockchain, which gets downloaded automatically upon joining the Bitcoin network. The blockchain has complete information about the addresses and their balances right from the genesis block to the most recently completed block.

BREAKING DOWN 'Blockchain'

The blockchain is seen as the main technological innovation of Bitcoin, since it stands as proof of all the transactions on the network. A block is the 'current' part of a blockchain which records some or all of the recent transactions, and once completed goes into the blockchain as permanent database. Each time a block gets completed, a new block is generated. There is a countless number of such blocks in the blockchain. So are the blocks randomly placed in a blockchain? No, they are linked to each other (like a chain) in proper linear, chronological order with every block containing a hash of the previous block.

To use conventional banking as an analogy, the blockchain is like a full history of banking transactions. Bitcoin transactions are entered chronologically in a blockchain just the way bank transactions are. Blocks, meanwhile, are like individual bank statements.

Based on the Bitcoin protocol, the blockchain database is shared by all nodes participating in a system. The full copy of the blockchain has records of every Bitcoin transaction ever executed. It can thus provide insight about facts like how much value belonged a particular address at any point in the past.

The ever-growing size of the blockchain is considered by some to be a problem due to issues like storage and synchronization. On an average, every 10 minutes, a new block is appended to the block chain through mining.

Bitcoin network data

A blockchain — originally block chain — is a distributed database that maintains a continuously-growing list of ordered records called blocks. Each block contains a timestamp and a link to a previous block.:6 By design blockchains are inherently resistant to modification of the data - once recorded, the data in a block cannot be altered retroactively.

Blockchains are secure by design and an example of a distributed computing system with high byzantine fault tolerance. Decentralised consensus can therefore be achieved with a blockchain. This makes blockchains suitable for the recording of events, title, medical records and other records management activities, identity management, transaction processing and proving provenance. This offers the potential of mass disintermediation and vast repercussions for how global trade is conducted.

The first blockchain was conceptualised by Satoshi Nakamoto in 2008 and implemented the following year as a core component of the digital currency bitcoin, where it serves as the public ledger for all transactions. Through the use of a peer-to-peer network and a distributed timestamping server a blockchain database is managed autonomously. The invention of the blockchain for bitcoin made it the first digital currency to solve the double spending problem. The bitcoin design has been the inspiration for other applications.

History

Bitcoin transactions (January 2009 - September 2015)

First work on cryptographically secured chain of blocks was described in 1991 by Stuart Haber and W. Scott Stornetta. Followed by publications in 1996 by Ross J. Anderson and 1998 by Bruce Schneier and John Kelsey. In parallel there was work going on in 1998 by Nick Szabo working on a mechanism for a decentralized digital currency that he called bit gold. In 2000 Stefan Konst published a general theory for cryptographic secured chains and suggested a set of solutions for implementation.

The first blockchain was then conceptualised by Satoshi Nakamoto in 2008 and implemented the following year as a core component of the digital currency bitcoin, where it serves as the public ledger for all transactions. Through the use of a peer-to-peer network and a distributed timestamping server a blockchain database is managed autonomously. The invention of the blockchain for bitcoin made it the first digital currency to solve the double spending problem. The bitcoin design has been the inspiration for other applications.

The blockchain format was first used for bitcoin, as a solution to the problem of making a database both secure and not requiring a trusted administrator. The words block and chain were used separately in Satoshi Nakamoto's original paper in October 2008, and when the term moved into wider use it was originally block chain, before becoming a single word, blockchain, by 2016. In August 2014, the bitcoin blockchain file size reached 20 gigabytes in size.

As of 2014, "Blockchain 2.0" was a term referring to new applications of the distributed blockchain database. The Economist described one implementation of this second-generation programmable blockchain as coming with "a programming language that allows users to write more sophisticated smart contracts, thus creating invoices that pay themselves when a shipment arrives or share certificates which automatically send their owners dividends if profits reach a certain level."

In 2016, the central securities depository of the Russian Federation (NSD) announced a pilot project based on blockchain technology. Various regulatory bodies in the music industry have started testing models that use blockchain technology for royalty collection and management of copyrights around the world. IBM opened a blockchain innovation research centre in Singapore in July 2016. A working group for the World Economic Forum met in November 2016 to discuss the development of governance models related to blockchain. According to Accenture an application of the diffusion of innovations theory suggests that in 2016 blockchains attained a 13.5% adoption rate within financial services, therefore reaching the early adopters phase. In 2016, industry trade groups joined to create the Global Blockchain Forum, an initiative of the Chamber of Digital Commerce.

Description

Blockchain is a secured way of online transaction. A blockchain is a decentralized digital ledger that records transactions on thousands of computers globally in such a way that the registered transactions cannot be altered retrospectively. They are authenticated by mass collaboration powered by collective self-interests. The result is a robust workflow where participants' uncertainty regarding data security is marginal. The use of a blockchain removes the characteristic of infinite reproducibility from a digital asset. It confirms that each unit of digital cash was spent only once, solving the long-standing problem of double spending. Blockchains have been described as a value-exchange protocol. This exchange of value can be completed more quickly, safely and cheaper with a blockchain. A blockchain can assign title rights because it provides a record that compels offer and acceptance. From the technical point of view a blockchain is a hashchain inside another hashchain.

A blockchain database consists of two kinds of records: transactions and blocks.Blocks hold batches of valid transactions that are hashed and encoded into a Merkle tree. Each block includes the hash of the prior block in the blockchain, linking the two. Variants of this format were used previously, for example in Git, and it is not by itself sufficient to *q*ualify as a blockchain. The linked blocks form a chain. This iterative process confirms the integrity of the previous block, all the way back to the original genesis block. Some blockchains create a new block as rapidly as every five seconds. As blockchains age they are said to grow in height. Blocks are structured by division into layers.

Sometimes separate blocks can be validated concurrently, creating a temporary fork. In addition to a secure hash based history, any blockchain has a specified algorithm for scoring different versions of the history so that one with a higher value can be selected over others. Blocks which are not selected for inclusion in the chain are called orphan blocks. Peers supporting the database don't have exactly the same version of the history at all times, rather they keep the highest scoring version of the database that they currently know of. Whenever a peer receives a higher scoring version (usually the old version with a single new block added) they extend or overwrite their own database and retransmit the improvement to their peers. There is never an absolute guarantee that any particular entry will remain in the best version of the history forever, but because blockchains are typically built to add the score of new blocks onto old blocks and there are incentives to only work on extending with new blocks rather than overwriting old blocks, the probability of an entry becoming superseded goes down exponentially as more blocks are built on top of it, eventually becoming very low.:ch. 08 For example, in a blockchain using the proof-of-work system, the chain with the most cumulative proof-of-work is always considered the valid one by the network. In practice there are a number of methods that can demonstrate a sufficient level of computation. Within a blockchain the computation is carried out redundantly rather than in the traditional segregated and parallel manner.

The blockchain is parsed by software to extract relevant information. The Nxt cryptocurrency community considered and dismissed a blockchain rollback in 2014 after a theft at a major exchange.

Chapter 2

Decentralization

By storing data across its network, the blockchain eliminates the risks that come with data being held centrally. Decentralised blockchains may use ad-hoc message passing and distributed networking. Its network lacks centralized points of vulnerability that computer hackers can exploit or any central point of failure. Blockchain security methods include the use of public-key cryptography.:5 A public key (a long, randomly-generated string of numbers) is an address on the blockchain. Bitcoins sent across the network are recorded as belonging to that address. A private key is like a password that gives its owner access to their digital assets or otherwise interact with the various capabilities that blockchains now support. Data stored on the blockchain is generally considered incorruptible.

Every node or miner in a decentralized system has a copy of the blockchain. Data quality is maintained by massive database replication and computational trust. No centralized "official" copy exists and no user is "trusted" more than any other. Transactions are broadcast to the network using software. Messages are delivered on a best effort basis. Mining nodes validate transactions, add them to the block they're creating, and then broadcast the completed block to other nodes.:ch. 08 Blockchains use various time-stamping schemes, such as proof-of-work to serialize changes. Alternate consensus methods include proof-of-stake and proof of burn. As a decentralised blockchain grows it becomes at risk to node decentralization because computer resource requirements for nodes increase becoming more expensive to operate

Openness

Open blockchains are more user friendly compared to some traditional ownership records, which while open to the public still require physical access to view. Since all early blockchains were permissionless, controversy has arisen over whether permissioned databases of chained blocks of data should even be considered blockchains. An issue in this ongoing debate is whether a private system with verifiers tasked and authorized (permissioned) by a central authority should be considered a blockchain.

Proponents of permissioned or private chains argue that the term "blockchain" may be applied to any data structure that batches data into time-stamped blocks. These blockchains serve as a distributed version of multiversion concurrency control (MVCC) in databases. Just as MVCC prevents two transactions from concurrently modifying a single object in a database, blockchains prevent two transactions from spending the same single output in a blockchain.

Opponents say that permissioned systems resemble traditional corporate databases, not supporting decentralized data verification, and that such systems are not hardened against operator tampering and revision. The Harvard Business Review defines blockchain as a distributed ledger or database open to anyone, and Computerworld claims that "much of [blockchain hype] is nothing more than snake oil and spin"

Permissionless

The great advantage to an open, permissionless network is that guarding against bad actors is not required and no access control is needed. Gatekeeping is not possible.[citation needed] This means that applications can be added to the edge of the network without the approval or trust of others, using the blockchain as a transport layer. This openness allows researchers to examine real-time transaction data in a closed economic system.

Bitcoin and Ethereum currently secure their blockchain by requiring new entries including a proof of work. To prolong the blockchain, bitcoin uses Hashcash puzzles developed by Adam Back in the 1990s. Ethereum plans to switch to a proof-of-stake system in the future.

Financial companies have not prioritised decentralized blockchains. In 2016, venture capital investment for blockchain related projects was weakening in the USA but increasing in China. Bitcoin and Ethereum use open (public) blockchains. As of September 2016, bitcoin has the highest market capitalization while Ethereum is second.

Permissioned

Main article: Distributed ledger

Permissioned blockchains are emerging as open source protocols where openness and collaboration are encouraged. These will always have the ability to restrict who can participate in the consensus processes as well as who can transact. These private blockchains lack transparency. They do not rely on anonymous miners to validate transactions nor do they benefit from the network effect. Miners are vetted. The New York Times notes that many corporations are using blockchain networks "with private blockchains, independent of the public system."

Disadvantages

Nikolai Hampton pointed out in Computerworld that "There is also no need for a '51 percent' attack on a private blockchain, as the private blockchain (most likely) already controls 100 percent of all block creation resources. If you could attack or damage the blockchain creation tools on a private corporate server, you could effectively control 100 percent of their network and alter transactions however you wished." This has a set of particularly profound adverse implications during a financial crises or debt crises like the financial crisis of 2007–08, where politically powerful actors may make decisions that favor some groups at the expense of others. and that "The bitcoin blockchain is protected by the massive group mining effort. It's unlikely that any private blockchain will try to protect records using gigawatts of computing power — it's time consuming and expensive." She also said "Within a private blockchain there is also no 'race'; there's no incentive to use more power or discover blocks faster than competitors. This means that many in-house blockchain solutions will be nothing more than cumbersome databases

Applications

While there is potential to transform business operating models there are few operational products maturing from proof of concept. The use of blockchains promises to be able to bring significant efficiencies to global supply chains although many observers remain skeptical. Some analysts, such as Steve Wilson from Constellation Research believe the technology has been hyped with unrealistic claims. In order to mitigate risk businesses are reluctant to place blockchain at the core of the business structure. Blockchains are a technology that may be integrated into multiple areas. It is a disruptive innovation because it allows businesses to use to new methods of processing digital transactions. Examples include a payment system and digital currency, facilitating crowdsales, or implementing prediction markets and generic governance tools.[citation needed] Blockchains are expected to disrupt the cloud computing industry although practical technical issues remain as obstacles.

Blockchains can be thought of as an automatically notarised ledger. They alleviate the need for a trust service provider and are predicted to result in less capital being tied up in disputes. Blockchains have the potential to reduce systemic risk and financial fraud. They automate processes which were previously time-consuming and done manually such as the incorporation of businesses. In theory, it would be possible to collect taxes, conduct conveyancing and provide risk management with blockchains.

Major applications of blockchain include cryptocurrencies—including bitcoin, BlackCoin, Dash, and Nxt—and blockchain platforms—Factom as a distributed registry, Gems for decentralized messaging, MaidSafe for decentralized applications, Storj for a distributed cloud, and Tezos for decentralized voting.:94 Frameworks and trials such as the one at the Sweden Land Registry aim to demonstrate the effectiveness of the blockchain at speeding land sale deals. The Republic of Georgia is piloting a blockchain-based property registry. The Ethical and Fair Creators Association uses blockchain to help startups protect their authentic ideas.

New distribution methods for the insurance industry such as peer-to-peer insurance, parametric insurance and microinsurance following the adoption of blockchain. Banks are interested in this technology because it has potential to speed up back office settlement systems. The sharing economy and IoT are also set to benefit from blockchains because they involve many collaborating peers. Online voting is another application of the blockchain. Blockchains are being used to develop information systems for medical records which increases interoperability. In theory legacy disparate systems can be completely replaced with blockchains. Blockchains are being developed for data storage, publishing texts and identifying the origin of digital art.

The Big Four

Each of the Big Four accounting firms are testing blockchain technologies in various formats. Ernst and Young has provided digital wallets to all employees, has installed a Bitcoin ATM in their office in Switzerland, and accepts Bitcoin as payment for all its consulting services. Mark Stalder, CEO of Ernst and Young Switzerland stated ""We don't only want to talk about digitalization, but also actively drive this process together with our employees and our clients. It is important to us that everybody gets on board and prepares themselves for the revolution set to take place in the business world through blockchains, two smart contracts and digital currencies."

PWC, Deloitte, and KPMG have taken a different path than Ernst & Young and are all testing private blockchains.

Smart contracts

Blockchain-based smart contracts are currently in development. One of the main objectives of a smart contract is automated escrow. The IMF believes blockchains could reduce moral hazards and optimize the use of contracts in general. Due to the lack of widespread use their legal status is unclear.

Some blockchain implementations could enable the coding of contracts that will execute when specified conditions are met. A blockchain smart contract would be enabled by extensible programming instructions which both define and execute an agreement. For example, Ethereum is an open source blockchain project that was built specifically to realize this possibility by implementing a Turing-complete programming language capability to implement such contracts.:ch. 11 As of January 2016, smart contract systems are not being used for ether. One of the more advanced projects is the Lightning Network by Blockstream.

Sidechains

One of the most important developments in the blockchain industry has been development of sidechains operating on a

2-way peg system. A sidechain is also blockchain that runs and operates akin to the main Blockchain network. The basic function of a sidechain is to amplify the functionality of the main blockchain by allowing a friction free transaction network back and forth the main blockchain.

Sidechains are decentralized, peer-to-peer networks that enhance the performance of a given blockchain network by adding features such as high security, lower risk, and efficient performance along with minimizing the storage space and operating length of the main blockchain. This enables global systems of value exchange with zero third party interference. And further, it allows developers to come up with new applications without a risk.

Two-way Pegging

A two-way pegging is a system that explains transfer of Bitcoins or cryptocurrencies, in general from the main blockchain to the sidechain and vice-versa.

Well, to your surprise, this transfer is a "mirage" and the currencies are not really transferred from the main chain to the sidechain. How it actually works is that a certain amount of tokens (to be transferred) is blocked in the main blockchain an d the same amount of tokens are unlocked in the sidechain. When the tokens in the main blockchain are unlocked, the one's in the secondary chain is locked again.

However, this assumption can be correctly realized if certain assumptions are taken into considerations. For instance,

We need to assume that the participants in a two-way peg are honest.

The main blockchain has not been censored at all.

The party that holds the custody of the licked tokens is also honest.

If these assumptions do not hold good, the two-peg will deploy a double-spend which is obviously vindictive.

Sidechains as special case of two-way pegging

When a blockchain does not want to put the bear down to numerous third parties, they administer another blockchain its premises and regard it as sidechain. This sidechain follows a protocol drawn out by solidarity.These sidechains are made to comprehend the consensus system of main blockchain and can thus are able to autonomously release tokens when given proof of a lock transaction in the main blockchain.

Shortcomings of sidechains

Public blockchains usually lack settlement finality (directives that apply to final payment and security settlement issues). If this feature stands missing in the sidechains, there is negligible assurance for secure locking of the tokens it them.

Besides, settlement finality, it requires entanglement (reversal of the lock transaction in the primary blockchain implies the reversal of the unlock transaction in the secondary blockchain).

Sidechains in Bitcoin requires a soft-fork or hard-fork to add new complex opcodes. Blockstream proposal is currently incomplete and does not address the validation of proof-of-work.

Applications

The Harvard Business Review conducted a two-year research project exploring how blockchain technology can securely move and store host "money, titles, deeds, music, art, scientific discoveries, intellectual property, and even votes". Furthermore, major portions of the financial industry are implementing distributed ledgers for use in banking, and according to a September 2016 IBM study, this is occurring faster than expected. The credit and debits payments company MasterCard has added three blockchain-based APIs for programmers to use in developing both P2P and B2B payment systems

Other uses

Blockchain technology can be used to create a permanent, public, transparent ledger system for compiling data on sales, storing rights data by authenticating copyright registration, and tracking digital use and payments to content creators, such as musicians. Imogen Heap's Mycelia service allowing managers to use a blockchain for tracking high-value parts moving through a supply chain was launched as a concept in July 2016. Everledger, "building systems to record the movement of diamonds from mines to jewelry stores", is one of the inaugural clients of IBM's blockchain-based tracking service

Chapter 3

Is blockchain technology the new internet?

The blockchain is an undeniably ingenious invention – the brainchild of a person or group of people known by the pseudonym, Satoshi Nakamoto. But since then, it has evolved into something greater and the main question every single person is asking is: What is Blockchain?

By allowing digital information to be distributed but not copied, blockchain technology created the backbone of a new type of internet. Originally devised for the digital currency, Bitcoin, the tech community is now finding other potential uses for the technology.

Bitcoin has been called "digital gold," and for a good reason. To date, the total value of the currency is close to $9 billion US.

And blockchains can make other types of digital value. Like the internet (or your car), you don't need to know how the blockchain works to use it. However, having a basic knowledge of this new technology shows why it's considered revolutionary.

What is Blockchain Technology?

"The blockchain is an incorruptible digital ledger of economic transactions that can be programmed to record not just financial transactions but virtually everything of value."

A distributed database

Picture a spreadsheet that is duplicated thousands of times across a network of computers. Then imagine that this network is designed to regularly update this spreadsheet and you have a basic understanding of the blockchain.

Information held on a blockchain exists as a shared — and continually reconciled — database. This is a way of using the network that has obvious benefits. The blockchain database isn't stored in any single location, meaning the records it keeps are truly public and easily verifiable. No centralized version of this information exists for a hacker to corrupt. Hosted by millions of computers simultaneously, its data is accessible to anyone on the internet.

To go in deeper with the Google spreadsheet analogy I would like you to read this piece from a blockchain specialist.

Blockchain as Google Docs

What is Blockchain Technology? A step-by-step guide than anyone can understand

"The traditional way of sharing documents with collaboration is to send a Microsoft Word document to another recipient, and ask them to make revisions to it. The problem with that scenario is that you need to wait until receiving a return copy before you can see or make other changes because you are locked out of editing it until the other person is done with it. That's how databases work today. Two owners can't be messing with the same record at once.That's how banks maintain money balances and transfers; they briefly lock access (or decrease the balance) while they make a transfer, then update the other side, then re-open access (or update again).With Google Docs (or Google Sheets), both parties have access to the same document at the same time, and the single version of that document is always visible to both of them. It is like a shared ledger, but it is a shared document. The distributed part comes into play when sharing involves a number of people.

Imagine the number of legal documents that should be used that way. Instead of passing them to each other, losing track of versions, and not being in sync with the other version, why can't *all* business documents become shared instead of transferred back and forth? So many types of legal contracts would be ideal for that kind of workflow.

You don't need a blockchain to share documents, but the shared documents analogy is a powerful one."

Durability and robustness

Blockchain technology is like the internet in that it has a built-in robustness. By storing blocks of information that are identical across its network, the blockchain cannot:

Be controlled by any single entity.

Has no single point of failure.

Bitcoin was invented in 2008. Since that time, the Bitcoin blockchain has operated without significant disruption. (To date, any of problems associated with Bitcoin have been due to hacking or mismanagement. In other words, these problems come from bad intention and human error, not flaws in the underlying concepts.)

The internet itself has proven to be durable for almost 30 years. It's a track record that bodes well for blockchain technology as it continues to be developed.

"As revolutionary as it sounds, Blockchain truly is a mechanism to bring everyone to the highest degree of accountability. No more missed transactions, human or machine errors, or even an exchange that was not done with the consent of the parties involved. Above anything else, the most critical area where Blockchain helps is to guarantee the validity of a transaction by recording it not only on a main register but a connected distributed system of registers, all of which are connected through a secure validation mechanism."

Transparent and incorruptible

The blockchain network lives in a state of consensus, one that automatically checks in with itself every ten minutes. A kind of self-auditing ecosystem of a digital value, the network reconciles every transaction that happens in ten-minute intervals. Each group of these transactions is referred to as a "block". Two important properties result from this:

Transparency

data is embedded within the network as a whole, by definition it is public.

It cannot be corrupted

altering any unit of information on the blockchain would mean using a huge amount of computing power to override the entire network.

In theory, this could be possible. In practice, it's unlikely to happen. Taking control of the system to capture Bitcoins, for instance, would also have the effect of destroying their value.

What is Blockchain Technology? A step-by-step guide than anyone can understand

"Blockchain solves the problem of manipulation. When I speak about it in the West, people say they trust Google, Facebook, or their banks. But the rest of the world doesn't trust organizations and corporations that much — I mean Africa, India, the Eastern Europe, or Russia. It's not about the places where people are really rich. Blockchain's opportunities are the highest in the countries that haven't reached that level yet."

Chapter 4

A network of nodes

A network of so-called computing "nodes" make up the blockchain.

What is Blockchain Technology? A step-by-step guide than anyone can understand

Node

(computer connected to the blockchain network using a client that performs the task of validating and relaying transactions) gets a copy of the blockchain, which gets downloaded automatically upon joining the blockchain network.

Together they create a powerful second-level network, a wholly different vision for how the internet can function.

Every node is an "administrator" of the blockchain, and joins the network voluntarily (in this sense, the network is decentralized). However, each one has an incentive for participating in the network: the chance of winning Bitcoins.

Nodes are said to be "mining" Bitcoin, but the term is something of a misnomer. In fact, each one is competing to win Bitcoins by solving computational puzzles. Bitcoin was the raison d'etre of the blockchain as it was originally conceived. It's now recognized to be only the first of many potential applications of the technology.

There are an estimated 700 Bitcoin-like cryptocurrencies (exchangeable value tokens) already available. As well, a range of other potential adaptations of the original blockchain concept are currently active, or in development.

"Bitcoin has the same character a fax machine had. A single fax machine is a doorstop. The world where everyone has a fax machine is an immensely valuable thing."

The idea of decentralization

By design, the blockchain is a decentralized technology.

Anything that happens on it is a function of the network as a whole. Some important implications stem from this. By creating a new way to verify transactions aspects of traditional commerce could become unnecessary. Stock market trades become almost simultaneous on the blockchain, for instance — or it could make types of record keeping, like a land registry, fully public. And decentralization is already a reality.

A global network of computers uses blockchain technology to jointly manage the database that records Bitcoin transactions. That is, Bitcoin is managed by its network, and not any one central authority. Decentralization means the network operates on a user-to-user (or peer-to-peer) basis. The forms of mass collaboration this makes possible are just beginning to be investigated.

Who will use the blockchain?

As web infrastructure, you don't need to know about the blockchain for it to be useful in your life.

Currently, finance offers the strongest use cases for the technology. International remittances, for instance. The World Bank estimates that over $430 billion US in money transfers were sent in 2015.

The blockchain potentially cuts out the middleman for these types of transactions. Personal computing became accessible to the general public with the invention of the Graphical User Interface (GUI), which took the form of a "desktop". Similarly, the most common GUI devised for the blockchain are the so-called "wallet" applications, which people use to buy things with Bitcoin, and store it along with other cryptocurrencies.

Transactions online are closely connected to the processes of identity verification. It is easy to imagine that wallet apps will transform in the coming years to include other types of identity management.

Enhanced security

By storing data across its network, the blockchain eliminates the risks that come with data being held centrally.

Its network lacks centralized points of vulnerability that computer hackers can exploit. Today's internet has security problems that are familiar to everyone. We all rely on the "username/password" system to protect our identity and assets online. Blockchain security methods use encryption technology.

The basis for this are the so-called public and private "keys". A "public key" (a long, randomly-generated string of numbers) is a users' address on the blockchain. Bitcoins sent across the network gets recorded as belonging to that address. The "private key" is like a password that gives its owner access to their Bitcoin or other digital assets. Store your data on the blockchain and it is incorruptible. This is true, although protecting your digital assets will also require safeguarding of your private key by printing it out, creating what's referred to as a paper wallet.

A second-level network

With blockchain technology, the web gains a new layer of functionality.

Already, users can transact directly with one another — Bitcoin transactions in 2016 averaged over $200,000 US per day. With the added security brought by the blockchain new internet business are on track to unbundle the traditional institutions of finance.

Goldman Sachs believes that blockchain technology holds great potential especially to optimize clearing and settlements, and could represent global savings of up to $6bn per year.

2017 will be a pivotal year for blockchain tech. Many of the startups in the space will either begin generating revenue – via providing products the market demands/values – or vaporize due to running out of cash. In other words, 2017 should be the year where there is more implementation of products utilizing blockchain tech, and less talk about blockchain tech being the magical pixie dust that can just be sprinkled atop everything. Of course, from a customers viewpoint, this will not be obvious as blockchain tech should dominantly be invisible – even as its features and functionality improve peoples'/business' lives. I personally am familiar with a number of large-scale blockchain tech use cases that are launching soon/2017. This implementation stage, which 2017 should represent, is a crucial step in the larger adoption of blockchain tech, as it will allow skeptics to see the functionality, rather than just hear of its promise."

Web 3.0

The blockchain gives internet users the ability to create value and authenticate digital information. What new business applications will result?

Smart contracts

Distributed ledgers enable the coding of simple contracts that will execute when specified conditions are met. Ethereum is an open source blockchain project that was built specifically to realize this possibility. Still in its early stages, Ethereum has the potential to leverage the usefulness of blockchains on a truly world-changing scale.

At the technology's current level of development, smart contracts can be programmed to perform simple functions. For instance, a derivative could be paid out when a financial instrument meets certain benchmark, with the use of blockchain technology and Bitcoin enabling the payout to be automated.

The sharing economy

With companies like Uber and AirBnB flourishing, the sharing economy is already a proven success. Currently, however, users who want to hail a ride-sharing service have to rely on an intermediary like Uber. By enabling peer-to-peer payments, the blockchain opens the door to direct interaction between parties — a truly decentralized sharing economy results.

An early example, OpenBazaar uses the blockchain to create a peer-to-peer eBay. Download the app onto your computing device and you can transact with OpenBazzar vendors without paying transaction fees. The "no rules" ethos of the protocol means that personal reputation will be even more important to business interactions than it currently is on eBay.

Crowdfunding

Crowdfunding initiatives like Kickstarter and Gofundme are doing the advance work for the emerging peer-to-peer economy. The popularity of these sites suggests people want to have a direct say in product development. Blockchains take this interest to the next level, potentially creating crowd-sourced venture capital funds.

In 2016, one such experiment, the Ethereum-based DAO (Decentralized Autonomous Organization), raised an astonishing $200 million USD in just over two months. Participants purchased "DAO tokens" allowing them to vote on smart contract venture capital investments (voting power was proportionate to the number of DAO they were holding). A subsequent hack of project funds proved that the project was launched without proper due diligence, with disastrous consequences. Regardless, the DAO experiment suggests the blockchain has the potential to usher in "a new paradigm of economic cooperation."

Governance

By making the results fully transparent and publicly accessible, distributed database technology could bring full transparency to elections or any other kind of poll taking. Ethereum-based smart contracts help to automate the process.

The app, Boardroom, enables organizational decision-making to happen on the blockchain. In practice this means company governance becomes fully transparent and verifiable when managing digital assets, equity or information.

Supply chain auditing

Consumers increasingly want to know that the ethical claims companies make about their products are real. Distributed ledgers provide an easy way to certify that the backstories of the things we buy are genuine. Transparency comes with blockchain-based timestamping of a date and location — on ethical diamonds, for instance — that corresponds to a product number.

The UK-based Provenance offers supply chain auditing for a range of consumer goods. Making use of the Ethereum blockchain, a Provenance pilot project ensures that fish sold in Sushi restaurants in Japan has been sustainably harvested by its suppliers in Indonesia.

File storage

Decentralizing file storage on the internet brings clear benefits. Distributing data throughout the network protects files from getting hacked or lost.

Inter Planetary File System (IPFS) makes it easy to conceptualize how a distributed web might operate. Similar to the way a bittorrent moves data around the internet, IPFS gets rid of the need for centralized client-server relationships (i.e., the current web). An internet made up of completely decentralized websites has the potential to speed up file transfer and streaming times. Such an improvement is not only convenient. It's a necessary upgrade to the web's currently overloaded content-delivery systems.

Prediction markets

The crowdsourcing of predictions on event probability is proven to have a high degree of accuracy. Averaging opinions cancels out the unexamined biases that distort judgment. Prediction markets that pay out according to event outcomes are already active. Blockchains are a "wisdom of the crowd" technology that will no doubt find other applications in the years to come.

Still in Beta, the prediction market application Augur makes share offerings on the outcome of real world events. Participants can earn money by buying into the correct prediction. The more shares purchased in the correct outcome, the higher the payout will be. With a small commitment of funds (less than a dollar), anyone can ask a question, create a market based on a predicted outcome, and collect half of all transaction fees the market generates.

Protection of intellectual property

As is well known, digital information can be infinitely reproduced — and distributed widely thanks to the internet. This has given web users globally a goldmine of free content. However, copyright holders have not been so lucky, losing control over their intellectual property and suffering financially as a consequence. Smart contracts can protect copyright and automate the sale of creative works online, eliminating the risk of file copying and redistribution.

Mycelia uses the blockchain to create a peer-to-peer music distribution system. Founded by the UK singer-songwriter Imogen Heap, Mycelia enables musicians to sell songs directly to audiences, as well as licence samples to producers and divvy up royalties to songwriters and musicians — all of these functions being automated by smart contracts. The capacity of blockchains to issue payments in fractional cryptocurrency amounts (micropayments) suggests this use case for the blockchain has a strong chance of success.

Internet of Things (IoT)

What is the IoT? The network-controlled management of certain types of electronic devices — for instance, the monitoring of air temperature in a storage facility. Smart contracts make the automation of remote systems management possible. A combination of software, sensors, and the network facilitates an exchange of data between objects and mechanisms. The result increases system efficiency and improves cost monitoring.

The biggest players in manufacturing, tech and telecommunications are all vying for IoT dominance. Think Samsung, IBM and AT&T. A natural extension of existing infrastructure controlled by incumbents, IoT applications will run the gamut from predictive maintenance of mechanical parts to data analytics, and mass-scale automated systems management.

Neighbourhood Microgrids

Blockchain technology enables the buying and selling of the renewable energy generated by neighbourhood microgrids. When solar panels make excess energy, Ethereum-based smart contracts automatically redistribute it. Similar types of smart contract automation will have many other applications as the IoT becomes a reality.

Located in Brooklyn, Consensys is one of the foremost companies globally that is developing a range of applications for Ethereum. One project they are partnering on is Transactive Grid, working with the distributed energy outfit, LO3. A prototype project currently up and running uses Ethereum smart contracts to automate the monitoring and redistribution of microgrid energy. This so-called "intelligent grid" is an early example of IoT functionality.

Chapter 5

Identity management

There is a definite need for better identity management on the web. The ability to verify your identity is the lynchpin of financial transactions that happen online. However, remedies for the security risks that come with web commerce are imperfect at best. Distributed ledgers offer enhanced methods for proving who you are, along with the possibility to digitize personal documents. Having a secure identity will also be important for online interactions — for instance, in the sharing economy. A good reputation, after all, is the most important condition for conducting transactions online.

Developing digital identity standards is proving to be a highly complex process. Technical challenges aside, a universal online identity solution requires cooperation between private entities and government. Add to that the need to navigate legal systems in different countries and the problem becomes exponentially difficult. E Commerce on the internet currently relies on the SSL certificate (the little green lock) for secure transactions on the web. Netki is a startup that aspires to create a SSL standard for the blockchain. Having recently announced a $3.5 million seed round, Netki expects a product launch in early 2017.

AML and KYC

Anti-money laundering (AML) and know your customer (KYC) practices have a strong potential for being adapted to the blockchain. Currently, financial institutions must perform a labour intensive multi-step process for each new customer. KYC costs could be reduced through cross-institution client verification, and at the same time increase monitoring and analysis effectiveness.

startup Polycoin has an AML/KYC solution that involves analysing transactions. Those transactions identified as being suspicious are forwarded on to compliance officers. Another startup Tradle is developing an application called Trust in Motion (TiM). Characterized as an "Instagram for KYC", TiM allows customers to take a snapshot of key documents (passport, utility bill, etc.). Once verified by the bank, this data is cryptographically stored on the blockchain.

Data management

Today, in exchange for their personal data people can use social media platforms like Facebook for free. In future, users will have the ability to manage and sell the data their online activity generates. Because it can be easily distributed in small fractional amounts, Bitcoin — or something like it — will most likely be the currency that gets used for this type of transaction.

The MIT project Enigma understands that user privacy is the key precondition for creating of a personal data marketplace. Enigma uses cryptographic techniques to allow individual data sets to be split between nodes, and at the same time run bulk computations over the data group as a whole. Fragmenting the data also makes Enigma scalable (unlike those blockchain solutions where data gets replicated on every node). A Beta launch is promised within the next six months.

Land title registration

As Publicly-accessible ledgers, blockchains can make all kinds of record-keeping more efficient. Property titles are a case in point. They tend to be susceptible to fraud, as well as costly and labour intensive to administer.

A number of countries are undertaking blockchain-based land registry projects. Honduras was the first government to announce such an initiative in 2015, although the current status of that project is unclear. This year, the Republic of Georgia cemented a deal with the Bitfury Group to develop a blockchain system for property titles. Reportedly, Hernando de

Soto, the high profile economist and property rights advocate, will be advising on the project. Most recently, Sweden announced it was experimenting with a blockchain application for property titles.

Stock trading

The potential for added efficiency in share settlement makes a strong use case for blockchains in stock trading. When executed peer-to-peer, trade confirmations become almost instantaneous (as opposed to taking three days for clearance). Potentially, this means intermediaries — such as the clearing house, auditors and custodians — get removed from the process.

Numerous stock and commodities exchanges are prototyping blockchain applications for the services they offer, including the ASX (Australian Securities Exchange), the Deutsche Börse (Frankfurt's stock exchange) and the JPX (Japan Exchange Group). Most high profile because the acknowledged first mover in the area, is the Nasda**q**'s Lin**q**, a platform for private market trading (typically between pre-IPO startups and investors). A partnership with the blockchain tech company Chain, Linq announced the completion of it its first share trade in 2015. More recently, Nasdaq announced the development of a trial blockchain project for proxy voting on the Estonian Stock Market.

WTF Is The Blockchain? A Guide for Total Beginners

Blockchain: the single most confusing term since Bitcoin. Everyone has a vague idea of what it does. It's either the ultimate evolution of financial technologies, or a silly fad that can be summed up in the disconcerting phrase: "dogechain." In reality, major companies around the world have already shown favor to the burgeoning money exchange system and it may become harder and harder to stay away from the financial dark art.

In reality, it is all relatively easy to understand. The Blockchain is a public ledger where transactions are recorded and confirmed anonymously. It's a record of events that is shared between many parties. More importantly, once information is entered, it cannot be altered. So, if the blockchain is the public record, what is being recorded? What are all of these "transactions"?

Cryptocurrencies, like bitcoin, are currencies that exist solely in digital. There are no physical golden coins with a big "B" on them. Moreover, owning these non-real coins entails a new idea of "ownership." You don't literally have it in your hands, or even in your bank account, but you have the ability to transfer "ownership" to someone else simply by creating a record in the blockchain. Rather than using bills, your transfer is pure data.

Where exactly is this chain located? Due to the open nature of cryptocurrencies, and the importance of the public having access to other blocks, the blockchain isn't located on just one guy's large computer. For example, the bitcoin blockchain is actually managed by distributed nodes. These nodes all have a copy of the entire blockchain. Nodes will forever come and go, synchronizing their own copies of the chain with those of other users. By distributing copies and access, the chain can't simply "go down," or disappear. It's a decentralized system that is both sturdy and secure.

All of your dogecoins are in a row, but what do you do with them? Whether you're using them IRL or online, the blockchain makes it happen. There are many reasons people are falling in love with cryptocurrencies: it's anonymous, decentralized, and there are no fees or third parties trying to grab a percentage. However, if there were absolutely no regulations in place, the new currency would quickly become a greedfest of users trying to screw each other over. The public nature of the blockchain means that anyone can check it. It is effectively anonymous, yet public, simultaneously, and it is in the best interest of users if it remains so.

A DIY Bitcoin mining rig, by Paul Anderson.

A DIY Bitcoin mining rig, by Paul Anderson.

You can accept and trade coins, or you can mine for them. Miners can spend thousands of dollars on the right equipment just to mine coin. But what do they really do? What miners do is quite similar to real-world miners in that they are actively looking for something. Their computer repeatedly works through complex calculations to find a very specific answer.

Miners solve problems, but how in the world is that helpful? Short story, miners are actually verifying that transactions posted by other users are legitimate, and the numbers all add up. Long story...

Miners collect transactions and put them into a single block. A block generally contains four pieces of information: a reference to the previous block, a summary of included transaction, a time stamp, and Proof of Work that went into creating the secure block. The blocks are strung together into a chain—a fluid chain that does not allow for any inconsistencies; this means there are no "bad cheques" in the system, and transactions entered are necessarily valid and can be processed. By checking the blockchain and confirming transactions, the entire system is effectively self-regulated and fully secure. No, that doesn't mean some kid cooped up in a basement can just click "okay" and confirm a billion dollar transfer. Blocks generally need numerous independent confirmations, and the equations are intended to be hard to crack. Not to mention, the hardware required is far more specialized than the average laptop. Finally, what's to stop someone from simply going back and editing existing blocks? Each block is securely hashed—meaning it is rendered into seeming gibberish and nearly impossible to invert or undo. Once it's in the blockchain, it's there forever.

A rough idea of what a block chain may look like, courtesy of Yevgeniy Brikman

A rough idea of what a block chain may look like, courtesy of Yevgeniy Brikman

So, why waste time and resources helping other people, or the blockchain? Why not let someone else do all that "confirmation stuff," while you just mine? Because, you don't necessarily have a choice. Confirmation of the blockchain is central to mining. It's part of the actual mining process; however, miners are generally given incentives. For example, after solving a problem (and creating a new hash) they are rewarded with coins.

Will you be seeing a blockchain-styled ledger in your future? Short answer: oh yes. Blockchain and cryptocurrencies have caused quite a stir over the past years. However, it seems their real importance has yet to be fully realized. The future isn't just in businesses around the globe sporting happy "Now Accepting Bitcoins" signs, but rather emerging companies (and revolutionary existing ones, too) finding new uses for the cutting edge technology. VC firms and investors are placing their bets on the blockchain because there is untapped potential. Identity management, international contracts, and all sorts of complicated bank transactions can be greatly altered with the public ledger system. The process could (in an ideal world) work seamlessly, crossing boundaries where banks, logistics or a plethora of other obstacles once existed. They could be combined with the Internet of Things to create a more connected and automated world. Future companies may be able to absorb mountains of new data, or even digitize real-world things that are hard to quantify. Unfortunately, many big companies are remaining mum on the studies in the blockchain field for obvious reasons.

However, it is public knowledge that nine major banks (including JP Morgan and Goldman Sachs) recently joined a partnership to develop blockchain technologies. That's not to say major companies are getting in on the cryptocurrency game; rather, they realize that the blockchain system, itself, could be a powerful tool for efficiency. With a system as versatile and secure as the blockchain, there may many unexpected innovations in the coming months and years.

All you need to know about blockchain, explained simply

Many people know it as the technology behind Bitcoin, but blockchain's potential uses extend far beyond digital currencies.

Its admirers include Bill Gates and Richard Branson, and banks and insurers are falling over one another to be the first to work out how to use it.

So what exactly is blockchain, and why are Wall Street and Silicon Valley so excited about it?

What is blockchain?

Currently, most people use a trusted middleman such as a bank to make a transaction. But blockchain allows consumers and suppliers to connect directly, removing the need for a third party.

Using cryptography to keep exchanges secure, blockchain provides a decentralized database, or "digital ledger", of transactions that everyone on the network can see. This network is essentially a chain of computers that must all approve an exchange before it can be verified and recorded.

How does it work in practice?

In the case of Bitcoin, blockchain stores the details of every transaction of the digital currency, and the technology stops the same Bitcoin being spent more than once.

Why is it so revolutionary?

The technology can work for almost every type of transaction involving value, including money, goods and property. Its potential uses are almost limitless: from collecting taxes to enabling migrants to send money back to family in countries where banking is difficult.

Blockchain could also help to reduce fraud because every transaction would be recorded and distributed on a public ledger for anyone to see.

Who is using it?

In theory, if blockchain goes mainstream, anyone with access to the internet would be able to use it to make transactions.

Currently only a very small proportion of global GDP (around 0.025%, or $20 billion) is held in the blockchain, according to a survey by the World Economic Forum's Global Agenda Council.

But the Forum's research suggests this will increase significantly in the next decade, as banks, insurers and tech firms see the technology as a way to speed up settlements and cut costs.

Companies racing to adapt blockchain include UBS, Microsoft, IBM and PwC. The Bank of Canada is also experimenting with the technology.

A report from financial technology consultant Aite estimated that banks spent $75 million last year on blockchain. And Silicon Valley venture capitalists are also *q*ueuing up to back it.

How I Explained Blockchain to My Grandmother

My grandmother likes to stay informed and recently told me: << I read on the magazine a few days ago about something called "blockchain". Everybody seems to have fallen in love with it so it must be something important. Unfortunately the article was full of technical jargon and I could not understand a thing. Do you know what it is? >>. << Yes, of course. >> was my prompt answer. << Good. Could you explain it to me? >>. She must have seen my face because she generously added: << Of course if you have time now. >> At that point I was caught between reluctance to give an explanation that could have only increased her confusion, and self-pride that told me I could do it. The latter won. So I took courage and started what would have turned into a lesson for life.

<< Assume all you have is a $100 bill to buy goods in a shopping mall. At the checkout you say that you will send an email promising to pay $100, with the email representing a promise to pay (i.e., an "electronic I.O.U."). The merchant happily accepts the email and goes to the bank. The bank also accepts the email and credits $100 to the merchant's account.

Sounds odd? Certainly for one reason: assuming just for one second that all happens as described, what is it of your $100 bill? It's still in your wallet. So does that mean you can buy goods for more than you have by simply sending emails? Too good to be true. However, believe it or not, the transaction can happen (and indeed it does in the real world- just have some patience and we'll get there).

To understand how this could ever be possible let's add a group of customers in the mall. Now, when you say that you will send the email I.O.U. the people will ask to receive the same email. There are some "special" customers in the crowd that will compete to be the first to validate the email (e.g., the sender, the receiver, the exchanged amount, the real possession of the claimed amount). Once they validate it, the content becomes "true" for all. But wait a minute: Since all "special" customers in the mall will want their validation to become "the" version of the truth, which one should you follow?

All special participants follow a rule (that is, a "protocol"): The first to solve an electronic puzzle, say a Sudoku, wins the race. As we all know a Sudoku is *q*uite a hard nut to crack, but the solution is easy to check. The winner is compensated for the hard work to solve the Sudoku. There is an incentive for the contenders to win the next time.[1] After checking that the puzzle is properly solved, contenders scrap their version and accept the winner's validated email as the "version of the truth". The email is then sent to all the people in the mall, which now all have the same copy, acknowledged as valid and immutable. With the version of the truth publicly accepted, everyone in the mall will know that you owe $100 to the shop and that the $100 bill in your hands is worth nothing.[2].

You now move to the next store in the mall and try to buy other goods worth $100. You make again the promise to pay via email. This time your offer will be refused. Why is that? Well, did I say that also the merchant received the email? This means that he perfectly knows that you don't have any money left. Before I forget again, both your bank and the merchant's bank are also in the loop. So the system is self-controlled and there's no need for any intermediary (e.g., a clearing house or the Central Bank) to tell parties how much each owns and if the transaction is acceptable.

What if instead you make the promise to pay to a clerk who has just been told that he was made redundant and that it's his last day of work? The clerk may want to retaliate. Why not give a lesson to his boss and accept a fake email payment from a stranger? In other words, what if he who receives your promise to pay has the intention to act maliciously and accepts an irregular transaction? Well, in this case the customers in the store (exactly those who received the first valid email) will raise a red flag (yes, we are in a world where people speak out). As long as 51% of customers say this (after all they all have the same copy of the "truth"), you will be refused to buy the goods. If the malicious clerk wants stubbornly to cheat the system, he will have to convince at least 51% of attendees who have no particular reason, nor vested interest, to buy his story. Hence the effort and energy to turn the system to his favour will be overwhelming and economically unfeasible. The system once again is self-controlling without the need of a central ruling authority.

To add even more "esoteric" elements to this already intricate scenario, when the merchant that received the valid I.O.U. will use it (or a portion of it) with some other party in the mall, the entire population in the mall will be informed exactly of what is happening. The history of the I.O.U. will never be lost and, at any time in the future, someone will be able- if duly authorized- to trace the transactions backwards and know that on that certain day at that certain time you passed your "electronic I.O.U." to buy goods for $100. It's as if the full history of the transaction was written in stone and will remain immutable thereafter.

This history repeats for all transactions between all parties in the mall. On a regular schedule the miners run the Sudoku and disseminate the validated I.O.U. emails. To recap, every participant in the mall (banks included) receive a copy of all the valid transactions since they entered the mall. If someone goes out and then returns later, they can still get the list of the transactions (only the valid ones, of course) during their absence. So at any time anyone in the mall has the latest updated list of all valid transactions (i.e., the "truth") from the beginning of time.

This simple (and rather silly- I apologize) story is to exemplify the features of the blockchain. In blockchain jargon, the "electronic I.O.U" is called "bitcoin". When you promise to pay $100 it's as if you are writing on a ledger that the title to redeem a value worth $100 is transferred from your account to the seller's account. If you try to spend it again (that is, to "double spend") someone will shout out loud that you are cheating. That's why the bank will accept the email I.O.U., because they know it belongs to a valid transaction.

You, the stores in the mall, the crowd of customers, the "special" participants that control the validity of all transactions, the banks that convert the I.O.U. into solid cash—and even the unfaithful clerks—all constitute the blockchain infrastructure. There is no centralized control; every party can transact with any other (that is, peer-to-peer) and it's the system itself that controls the validity of the exchanges. The "special" participants are called "miners", as their role is to "mine" and validate/ reject transactions following a schedule. Miners exist in the so called "Bitcoin" blockchain (also known as the "Satoshi" blockchain as a tribute to the inventor of bitcoins), while other forms of blockchain (e.g., Ripple) assign different roles to the validators of transactions. Miners collect valid transactions in a "block"[3]. Anyone can track back the history of a transaction because the blocks are connected (i.e., "chained"). So, in a nutshell, blockchain is a chain of bocks, each with a recorded ledger of validated electronic I.O.U.'s. All network members have a copy of the blockchain which represents the agreed version of the truth. >>

I then looked at my grandmother who had remained completely silent during the rather long explanation, asking if everything was clear. <<You make

difficult things look so simple. There is one thing, though, I need to ask. You said that I could pay using an email. >>. <<Yes, exactly. You just send an email and the payment is done. >> I answered, already proud of my performance. << So what is that you wanted to know? >> And she, with a candid smile: << What is an email? >>

[1] Some other malls in town may decide to use a different puzzle and different protocol (e.g., nobody gets paid), but the basic rule is that the version of truth descends from some evident activity performed by the claiming party.

[2] This part of the story is a bit stretched but use your imagination (I know I am abusing *q*uite much of it) to pretend the bill will magically disappear.

[3] In the Satoshi blockchain the collection schedule is every 10 minutes

Conclusion

Thank you again for downloading this book!

I hope this book was able to help you to UNDERSTAND how Effectively a blockchain is a kind of independent, transparent, and permanent database coexisting in multiple locations and shared by a community. This is why it's sometimes referred to as a mutual distributed ledger (MDL).

Finally, if you enjoyed this book, then I'd like to ask you for a favor, would you be kind enough to leave a review for this book on Amazon? It'd be greatly appreciated!

Thank you and good luck!

I truly do appreciate it!

Best Wishes,

Lee Maxwell

www.ingramcontent.com/pod-product-compliance
Lightning Source LLC
Chambersburg PA
CBHW070110210526
45170CB00013B/810